BLUEST NUDE

BLUEST NUDE

poems

AMA CODJOE

MILKWEED EDITIONS

Published 2022 by Milkweed Editions
Printed in the United States of America
Cover design by Mary Austin Speaker
Cover artwork by Simone Leigh: *Martinique*, 2020.
Glazed Stoneware; 62 x 53 x 44 inches; 157.5 x 134.6 x 111.8 cm.
© Simone Leigh, Courtesy Matthew Marks Gallery

22 23 24 25 26   5 4 3 2 1
First Edition

Library of Congress Cataloging-in-Publication Data

Names: Codjoe, Ama, 1979- author.
Title: Bluest nude : poems / Ama Codjoe.
Description: First edition. | Minneapolis, Minnesota : Milkweed
    Editions, 2022. | Summary: "Ama Codjoe's highly anticipated debut
    collection brings generous light to the inner dialogues of women as
    they bathe, create art, make and lose love. Each poem rises with the
    urgency of a fully awakened sensual life"-- Provided by publisher.
Identifiers: LCCN 2021057571 (print) | LCCN 2021057572 (ebook) |
    ISBN 9781571315427 (paperback) | ISBN 9781571317551 (ebook)
Subjects: LCGFT: Poetry.
Classification: LCC PS3603.O2954 B58 2022 (print) | LCC PS3603.
    O2954 (ebook) | DDC 811/.6--dc23/eng/20211222
LC record available at https://lccn.loc.gov/2021057571
LC ebook record available at https://lccn.loc.gov/2021057572

Milkweed Editions is committed to ecological stewardship. We strive to align
our book production practices with this principle, and to reduce the impact
of our operations in the environment. We are a member of the Green Press
Initiative, a nonprofit coalition of publishers, manufacturers, and authors
working to protect the world's endangered forests and conserve natural
resources. *Bluest Nude* was printed on acid-free 100% postconsumer-waste
paper by McNaughton & Gunn.

To *the most beautiful*

Contents

"To name ourselves rather than be named
we must first see ourselves . . .
So long unmirrored in our true selves
we may have forgotten how we look."

—LORRAINE O'GRADY

BLUEST NUDE

I.

Blueprint

As I lay on the prickly grass, grasshoppers chattered
in my hair. I stroked the ground like a beard. No one
sang. The whole sky was watching. It's animal
piss in the dye pot that makes indigo blue. Blue
seeped out of me, but I wanted to forge it myself.
I was obsessed with making. The yellow leaves
browned; the sugar pine needles refused
to shed. I couldn't get the pigment right, it kept turning
to mud. I had attempted this before, making wine
from another's body, stamping and stomping
my grape-stained feet. When I rose, I left the print
of a woman behind. I noticed the pear tree, how it gave
without question; I asked anyway, was asking
again, collecting broken seashells and tiny
elephant figurines. I needed a herd of blue.
I soaked black beans for the color they left. My blue
was a habit, a kind of river I stepped into—sometimes
crossed—because it held the sky so perfectly.
I swung the axe. I swam with my arms.
I hammered nails—though crookedly. Timber
was my sacrum, timber were my metatarsals,
timber was my lungs' pink flesh, timber was my skull.
I was a blueprint, blue on blue, mapless
but for those warm bones and my red heart barking.
—And when I turned without making my skirt
a basket, when I turned from all the fallen
pears, the sky was full of shaking: wet
with river-water. It wasn't rain that fell—whatever it was
I collected in the cups of my hands.

On Seeing and Being Seen

I don't like being photographed. When we kissed
at a wedding, the night grew long and luminous.
You unhooked my bra. *A photograph*
passes for proof, Sontag says, *that a given thing*
has happened. Or you leaned back to watch
as I eased the straps from my shoulders.
Hooks and eyes. Right now, my breasts
are too tender to be touched. *Their breasts*
were horrifying, Elizabeth Bishop writes. Tell her
someone wanted to touch them. I am touching
the photograph of my last seduction. It is as slick
as a magazine page, as dark as a street
darkened by rain. When I want to remember
something beautiful, instead of taking
a photograph, I close my eyes.
I watched as you covered my nipple
with your mouth. Desire made you
beautiful. I closed my eyes.
Tonight, I am alone in my tenderness.
There is nothing in my hand except a certain
grasping. In my mind's eye, I am
stroking your hair with damp fingertips. This is exactly
how it happened. On the lit-up hotel bed,
I remember thinking, My body is a lens
I can look through with my mind.

Two Girls Bathing

I'm thirteen when my cousin teaches me
how to bathe. We carry buckets

from Auntie's kitchen, limping
to the pendulum of water swinging.

Undressed, we stand side by side
on the concrete floor. Carol's hands

don't handle like my mother's did:
propping me in the bathtub beside

my brothers, constructing an assembly line
of our limbs, as she lathered

and polished us clean. This was before
boys became unlike girls, before

our mother, whose flesh we ate,
whose nipples we cracked,

was exiled from us. Carol instructs me
wordlessly. In deliberate movements,

she rubs across her torso's cross
and sweeps beneath each breast.

I mimic her gestures: tipping the bucket
slightly, so as not to dirty the water.

I watch how easily she bares
her supple body. She wears her nakedness

like it's been woven from air.
Carol points to a spot on my back.

I resist the urge to hide my chest.
Tucked inside her is what hangs

from my brothers like pockets turned
inside out. I tilt my head like a mirror,

envy the gold beads hugging her waist,
and bring the washcloth to where I've missed:

not knowing when and from whom
I learned to be ashamed.

Marigolds of Fire

1.

He had a caribou's face. Once he let me
lick the sadness there. It tasted of salt

and moss-covered rocks. He grew the beard
of a mountain goat. He scaled the face

of a mountain. Lying beside him, I stared
into the face of faceless waters whose velvet

antlers cradled us. He wore a bison's
face. Sometimes he wallowed in the dust,

tossing his head from side to side,
wearing deep grooves into the braided

rug. Mornings, he refused to betray
his dreams. He had an antelope's face—I could

go on like this. I liked how he led me, almost
a shove, how he kissed me—mercy—how I

kissed him back: my back against the foyer
wall. Sometimes we called to each other

like birds. It wasn't ritual—how can I
explain—he laced his fingers, made his knees

a ladder. I braced myself on his backward horns.
I climbed him then, into the tree.

2.

In the end, we were delivered back

to the strange mud from which we crawled.

The bed gave us back, unastonished,

our aching, separate bodies.

This is skin, it told us. *Skin*, I wrote.

I would commit its meaning to memory.

3.

A football player slaps the butt
of a passing girl. She turns
to face a silvered hand dangling
from each player's wrist: windless
chimes. Under their helmets,
the teammates wear the same blank face.
—Can I tell you I wanted them all?

4.

In the beginning, there was blood or the threat

of blood. Formed from clay, we sought a fire

that could finish us. We sewed a garland

of marigolds. We ate good blossoms whole.

5.

He takes his coffee with cream
and sugar; she takes it black.
          She scans her wardrobe
for a dress. They respond to emails
and tidy their desks. At 4 am,
the garbage truck jostles her awake. He sleeps best
               on his side, on his back,
on his belly. He calls her lady. Though before she'd wince
at this term of endearment, she hears the word *babe*
slip out of her.
          It slips out of her mouth . . . His eyes
are tired. She has bags under her eyes. She waters
               the cactus in a slip. The sky
turns stormy. He forgets the umbrella. She wants
to storm out. He believes she'll leave. He forgets
to call. She calls him a name. She takes it
               back . . . He takes it black, no
sugar. He's confused. He wants a baby. She
winces. They rub their eyes. It was a slip. A mistake.
He packs his bags. She irons the sky-blue
dress. She can't stand his silences. The way he slips
in and out of her. The phone was on silent.
          The ringer was off. She removes the ring
from the tub . . . He sleeps
          on the couch, on his side. The sky
is a bath of coffee grounds. Her face is full
of clouds. His eye waters. Somewhere
near a marsh there's a starling roosting.
I'm saying the middle
          was filled with the end.

Labor
Manhattan, New York

The Upper West Side brims
with Black women heaving Bugaboo
strollers as if maneuvering horseless plows.
I'm walking up Broadway with a white friend
whose mother's food stamps we used
as kids to buy Sour Straws, barbecue
chips, and frosted pints of Cherry Garcia.
While we zigzag between pedestrians,
she argues that there may be as many
white, working-class nannies steering
double-wide strollers as Black.
It's hard to tell, she insists,
whether the white women caring
for white babies are laborers
or mothers. I know we use
the same word to describe work
and the work of giving birth.
Still, I'm tempted to call her bluff.
Today, I do not want children.
I recall instances when I've been mistaken
for mother. Like last May, when a man
clutching a fistful of blush roses
wished me Happy Mother's Day.
Or in a muggy subway car,
as the child beside me rested his head
on my arm. A nearby passenger's eyes
softened at our portrait.
I claimed the sleeping child then,
briefly, I claimed him.

More than once, I've held tightly
the hands of my twin nephews,
who could be confused
for each other—or as mine.
Together, we've waited near
the chasm of the street—gust of cars
stealing their reflections. I've spent hours,
brief minutes, tending to children
I in no way labored for—and then,
with some relief, I have let them go.

Poem After Betye Saar's *The Liberation of Aunt Jemima*

What if, Betye, instead of a rifle or hand
grenade—I mean, what if after
the loaded gun that takes two hands
to fire, I lay down the splintered broom
and the steel so cold it wets
my cheek? What if I unclench the valleys
of my fist, and lay down
the wailing baby?
Gonna burn the moon in a cast-iron skillet.
Gonna climb the men who, when they see my face, turn into
        stony mountains.
Gonna get out of the kitchen.
Gonna try on my nakedness like a silk kimono.
Gonna find me a lover who eats nothing but pussy.
Let the whites of my eyes roll, roll.
Gonna clench my toes.
Gonna purr beneath my own hand.
Gonna take down my hair.
Try on a crown of crow feathers.
Gonna roam the wide aisles of the peach grove, light dripping
        off branches like syrup, leaves brushing the fuzz on my
        arms.
—You dig?—
Gonna let the juice trickle down my chin.
Gonna smear the sun like war paint across my chest.
Gonna shimmy into a pair of royal blue bell-bottoms.
Gonna trample the far-out thunderclouds, heavy in their
        lightness.
Watch them slink away.
Gonna grimace. Gonna grin.
Gonna lay down my sword.

Pick up the delicate eggs of my fists.
Gonna jab the face that hovered over mine.
It's easy to find the lips, surrounded as they are in minstrel black.
Gonna bloody the head of every god, ghost, or swan who has torn
　　　　into me—pried me open with its beak.
Gonna catch my breath in a hunting trap.
Gonna lean against the ropes.
Gonna break the nose of mythology.
—Goodnight John-Boy—
Gonna ice my hands in April's stream.
Gonna scowl and scream and shepherd my hollering into a green
　　　　pasture.
Gonna mend my annihilations into a white picket fence.
Gonna whip a tornado with my scarlet handkerchief.
Spin myself dizzy as a purple-lipped drunkard.
Gonna lay down, by the riverside, sticky and braless in the
　　　　golden sand.
Ain't gonna study war no more.
Ain't gonna study war no more.
Ain't gonna study war no more.

Diamondback

Like an organ coiled
      deep inside or a lasso
of lightning and high
         noon, the rattlesnake
traveled the length
     of my spine, sunning itself
inside me. Then death—some
        call it *god*—drew a diamond
on the snake's back,
     and marked my chest
with feeling. How godly
       the two of us were, shaking
what was hollow.
     Dirt stained
the front of my blouse.
       I felt venom
rise in my ears. I rubbed myself
     against a rock,
turning my skin bronze
       and flawless. This is how
I became a woman,
     sun slithering
across my back,
       dust glittering my tongue,
the snake's tail whirring.

After the _____, I yearned to be reckless. To smash
a glass brought first to my lips. To privilege lust over
tomorrow. To walk naked down the middle of a two-lane
road. But, too late, without my bidding, life cracked open,
rushed, openmouthed, like a panting dog whose name
I did not call—my lips shut like a purse. The last man
I kissed was different than the last man I fucked.
We were so desperate then, the two of us, undone
by longing, drawing night from the cracks
inside us, drawing the night out, as long as we could,
until dawn broke like a beat egg and our heartbeats
quieted in private fatigue. I'd be lying if I said I don't recall
his name. The end of the world has ended, and desire is still
all I crave. Oh, to be a stone, sexless and impenetrable.
Over half of me is water, a river spilling into restless limbs,
the rest of me is a scalding heat like the asphalt under my feet.

Detail from "Poem After Betye Saar's *The Liberation of Aunt Jemima*"

And out of her gushing head, I witnessed
four fully-grown women spring forth
like winged beasts: the first woman
wore the charm of her unmasked hair
and a taken-for-granted beauty that made
her all the more enticing; the last woman
modeled an anonymous version of herself—
an "I" that didn't remind anyone
of anyone else, but who reminded Aunt Jemima
of freedom; the second woman brandished
a handheld mirror she spat on
then polished with the ruffled hem
of her apron, a mirror all the women,
except the last, gathered around
like campfire; and the second to last
woman carried a pink mulatto, squirming
on her hip—in the baby's hand a rattle,
in the rattle a shattered lightbulb,
in the filament, a portrait
of the child's father, who some say
Aunt Jemima tempted with her bottle-shaped
hips, but who was known to be monstrous—
a so-called god—and I beheld a sea
of blood, dark as syrup, oozing
from Aunt Jemima's neck,
and four women flying, without shoes
or wings, from her maternal, amber body.

Primordial Mirror

I was newly naked: aware of myself
as a separate self, distinct from dirt and bone.

I had not hands enough,
and so, finally, uncrossed my arms.

In trying to examine one body part,
I'd lose sight of another. I couldn't

imagine what I looked like during
the fractured angles of sex.

At the river's edge, it was impossible
to see all of myself at once.

I began to understand nakedness
as a feeling.

It was a snake, loose and green;
it was the snake skin, coiled and discarded.

The shedding chained itself
like a balloon ribboned to a child's wrist.

Morning's birdsong reminded me
of the sloughing off of skin.

The rumored beauty of my husband's first
wife never bothered me before.

I missed the sensation of being fixed
in amber. Then the hair in the comb,

fingernail clippings, the red mole on my
left breast grown suddenly bigger.

I perceived my likeness in everything:
the lines on my palm as the veins

of a leaf, my mind as a swarm of flies
humming over something sugary or dead,

my vulnerability as the buck
I'd kill, then wrap myself inside,

my hair as switchgrass, twine, and nest,
a roving cloud my every limb.

Le Sacre du printemps
after Pina Bausch

At this time of night, the theater is empty:
draped in its velvet robes, echoing with ghosts

and applause. I've been tossing and turning
all night, as headlights flash across the ceiling.

Inside the ornate opera house, it felt close to midnight—
bottomless, like tonight—though it was the middle

of the day when I arrived and the usher
escorted me to my seat. An ocean of dirt

covered the stage. The dancers performed
underneath and on top of Stravinsky's score.

With their bodies, they made another music:
full of lunges, panting, slaps, stomps,

and whatever sounds the body makes
when it yields to unyielding earth.

Men and women threw themselves on the floor
and into each other: smearing their skins

with dirt, violence, and sweat.
I am restless. Tonight, I remember

I vowed to feel as alive as the woman
who, in a rite of spring, must dance herself

to death. Hair frazzled, clothes soiled, the fated
woman fell to the earth then sprang back up,

slashing the air and contracting her body as if
she'd been punched repeatedly. She fell

and danced, danced and fell, until she collapsed
for the last time. —The stage went black.

How quickly I walked into the bright day,
leaving her there, behind me. On nights

like this one, when I'm crazed by wakefulness,
and darkness sacrifices itself, anxious limb

by anxious limb, into the day's endless mouth,
I steal the red dress from the dead woman's body

and dance wildly, with such abandon,
the room turns stained, swirling, terrible, pink.

After the _____, I had the urge to dance
on the president's grave. The dispossessed threw me
a belated quinceañera. My godmother wore a necklace
of the dictator's teeth. She sliced an upside-down cake, licked
her forefinger, and said, *You have mastered sadness, querida,*
may your rage be sticky and sweet. My father offered
his hand—this time I took it. We glided like
ballroom dancers across the red dirt floor. He wore
a grave expression. I embraced him tightly
so as to cloak my face. Instead of a toast, he handed me
a handkerchief wet with tears. My father circled
the guests silently, dabbing gently each of their cheeks.
This too was a dance unfolding. I folded the handkerchief
into a fist and raised my fist like a glass of champagne.
The pain in my father's eyes sparkled like the sequins
on my tattered gown. If it hadn't been so ugly,
it would've been beautiful. The party ended just as
the world had: with the sound of rain beating
against the earth and each of us on our hands
and knees, peering into pools of mud and thirst.

II.

She Said

Hello

Can you hear me

Can you hear me now

Hello

I can't hear you

I'm sorry you're breaking up

Is this better

Can you hear me now

Hello

Hello

Can you hear me now

Hello

*

And the said Agostino retorted that . . . [hole in page] and that he should find it, that otherwise he would have . . . [hole in page] for this ugly . . . [holes in page]

[[20. How long after it happened [did you tell]? Why didn't you tell it immediately, and, if immediately, why didn't you bring suit? Why have you said it now and what induced you to say it?]]

To the twentieth, she said

To the twenty-first, she said

To the twenty-second, she said

To the tenth one she answered as above

To the twelfth, she referred to the next one

And to the first [question] she answered

And while they were writing this down

To the third one she answered

To the thirteenth, she answered

To the eighth one she said

And the said summoned woman answered

*

FOOTNOTE 58: Hole in the page, one or two words missing.

FOOTNOTE 51: Hole in the page; three words missing.

I'm sorry you're breaking—

She was asked

She answered

FOOTNOTE 68: The page is torn; two or three words are missing at the beginning of the line, and a line or more is cut off at the bottom of the page.

The said summoned woman retorting

Can you—

FOOTNOTE 63: See ms. 10.

*

And while the guard tightened the said cords with a running string, the said woman began to say

Then the judge, having heard [all this], etc., terminated the interrogation and ordered that the witness be sent back to her house for the time being.

*

When considering this poem, I know the "I" is missing. Twelve years ago, on one occasion, [ ] was robbed, assaulted, and almost raped by the same man, a stranger.

*

Is this better

Footnote 26: Literally, "lying in his throat" (mentirà per la gola).

How about now

The connection is bad

Sorry

Hold on

Hold on

Literally, "lying in his throat"

How about now

How

repeating the above words over and over, and then saying,

o   sorry

                    breaking

                              Hell

o

          sorry

                    about

     no

                         now

                    o

Hell

                    He

                                        better

     hear

                              breaking

          break

                         better

be

          breaking

                                                  this

                              can't

                    me

the *hear* in hearing the *ear* the *he* the *he* in she the *sh* in shame the
me the shh in me the ssshhhh the *y* in saying the why the *say* the
said the sad the sad *i* the scared *i* terrified she tried to say the *test*
in testify the *be* in believed the *lie* the lived the silent *i* the why
in silence the shh in she the *she* before the space before the space
between *she* and *said* the *ears* in years the saying the said between

*

She added afterward voluntarily

She answered

She added afterward voluntarily

She added afterward

She added afterward voluntarily

She answered

She answered

She added afterward voluntarily

*

"At this point, I will do my best to answer your questions."

*

FOOTNOTE 70: Page is torn; a final line not legible.

III.

"It's essential that I do this work
and it's essential that I do it with *my* body."
—CARRIE MAE WEEMS

Posing Nude

after Living Room, Brownsville, Brooklyn
by Deana Lawson

If I were to choose a man to pose nude
with, it would be the ex whose hand
in mine, I couldn't distinguish
from my own—just as, studying
this photograph, it's hard to tell
the male's fingers, pressed
into a triangle, from the female's,
decorated by acrylic nails so long
they curve like a penis might.

This particular ex anticipated
my needs like a photographer considers
sources of light. He'd wrap me in a blanket
before opening the window
to smoke a cigarette. We gazed at each other
from a certain distance.
In choosing him, I choose
the feeling of waiting naked
beneath the throw, wanting nothing
but the last dashed ember—and next
his mouth sucking
my earlobes and neck.

In *Living Room*, a male figure bares
a tattooed chest, cuffed jeans,
and Timberlands. Behind him, a woman
sits, propped on the radiator. Leaning back,
he rests on her right breast.
The couple stares at the camera.

I know the composition is staged—
down to the cast-off shoes, askew
on the floor. A photograph tells truths
and lies. The couple pictured are not
lovers. Lawson asked the female subject
who she'd feel most comfortable
posing nude with: she chose a friend.

Years ago, my ex sent me nude photos.
At the time, he was living
with the woman he would later
marry. His face remains just
outside the frame. The subject
of the email read, "For Your Eyes Only."

In the only photograph of us I've kept,
I'm wearing a necklace. The clasp
will soon break. Tenderness closes
my eyes into lines. He stares at me
instead of the camera; his face breaks
into laughter. That night in bed,
after the picture was taken, a mosquito
worried past his ear. My mouth rested
on his chest. He woke bitten and swollen.

Burying Seeds

for Betty Shabazz

Who, when they killed her husband, was carrying
twin girls—not in her arms, but in an armless
sea, with bits of blood as food. She covered

her daughters in the waters of her body.
She covered her daughters in the rooms
her body built, pressed against the wooden

floor of the Audubon Ballroom. She must have
cried, as my mother did, when she stuttered, *Twins?*
into the paper gown of the hospital room.

The body longs for its double. Even twins
stretch long their arms toward other strangers.
The first time I visited a mosque, I was surprised

to be separated from my father and brothers.
I sat, with the women and girls, alone.
From across the aisle, I stared at the men

longingly. As a child, I asked my preschool teacher
why I couldn't play outside, shirtless like
the boys. It was a hot day. Before she could answer,

I relented, wearing my favorite undershirt—the one
with Archie, Betty, and Veronica—chasing
my sun-kissed brothers across the playground.

Lately, when I glimpse my nakedness in the half
mirror above the bathroom sink, I'm looking
at the photograph of Pauline Lumumba baring

her breasts as a sign of mourning. The widow's
breasts and mine hang like four weeping eyes,
without titillation, fertility, or innocence.

I wanted to write a poem for Betty Shabazz
because her high cheekbones and luminous
eyes are like a BaKongo mask breathed

into with life. After her husband's lifeless
body was wrapped in white linen and covered
by the words: *what we place in the ground*

is no more now a man—but a seed—she took
one last look at him who *had* smiled at her
and touched, countless times, her unveiled face.

My mother did not wear a veil on her wedding day.
Eighteen years after their divorce, my father
fidgets with the gold band she slid along his finger.

As she made a circle with her thumb and forefinger,
shimmying the ring over my father's knuckle,
which words did her mind circle over: *worse* or *better*

death or *death?* That night, did my mother bunch
the hotel bedsheet in one hand like a nosegay?
Did she allow it—another white dress—to drag,

crumpled, behind her? The vows we promise
one another are veils through which we envision
the future; we enact our dreams using a vision

clouded by tulle and lace. Grief-stricken, Betty Shabazz
said of her husband's assassination, *Well, it finally
happened.* Weeks prior, she had taken to wearing

her husband's hat for comfort and continued to do so
after he died. I want a desire that could be mistaken
for grief to cloud my face, to make me shudder, to twist

my mouth into a cry. Once, I shared a bed with a man
who, as a boy, heard his parents' lovemaking. *I was
confused,* he admitted, *it sounded like they were in pain.*

Grief is the bride of every good thing, Betty Shabazz
reminds me. I'm wearing a veil the shape of a waterfall,
which is also the shape of my mother's dress, falling

from her shoulders. Through its fabric, I can see a cloud
turning into a horse and a plane that could be a star—
a star that might be a planet. It's hard to tell from here,

wrapped in the caul of the present, fixed on this plot
of grass, with so many seeds buried underground,
and winter—forged into a circle—threatening never to end.

At the Fish House
Captiva, Florida

I'm contemplating the difference between anger
      and resentment, but I'm interrupted each time
a brown pelican crashes into the water, more recklessly,
         it seems, because of the approaching storm.

The water turns field and beast, like the mind
      which is also like the body: tractor of memory
raking the ground you become when loss,
         proof of your heart, confounds you. Another dives.

I can't remember what it feels like to snare
      my tongue in someone's mouth, or the date
my grandfather died. It was a Tuesday
         in September. My mother woke me from stilted sleep.

Pelican chicks dive so deeply inside a mother or father's
      gular pouch the chicks were thought to be
cannibals, feeding on the blood of their parent's breast.
         To my right, lightning like a thought cut short.

From far away the pelican spots the menhaden,
      which my eye can't distinguish from water.
I get no further than the question. A cold wind
         rushes from my eyes. I go inside, shut the windows.

Why I Left the Garden

After I lost my breast, I became a woman
sutured by a kind of knowledge.

All day I moved as if walking was no different
from falling. I owned the pot holes
and the riddled sky. I owned nothing at all.

Even from far away,
I could hear the record skipping.
Time was running out
of hands. Of faces.

The first time a lover traced
my scar, fingered its river
and kissed its groove, I woke early
the next morning and, quietly, I left.

After the _____, I mothered my mother,
became grandmother to myself, distant and tender,
temples turning gray. The whole world cascaded
past my shoulders, like the hair self-hatred taught me
to crave—though all my Barbie dolls were Black.
And the Cabbage Patch Kid my grandmother placed
under the artificial Christmas tree, sprinkled with tinsel,
in Memphis, Tennessee, the city where my mother waited
for her first pair of glasses in the Colored Only
waiting room. She said the world changed
from black-and-white to Technicolor that day.
My mother watches TV as I roll her hair. She sits
between my legs. I've never birthed a child. I have
fondled the crown of a lover's head, my thighs framing
his dark brown eyes. I entered the world excised
from my mother's womb. Her scar is a mark
the color of time. I am my mother's weeping
wound. On my last birthday, I cried into bathwater. I hid
my tears from my mother because that's what mothers do.

Facing Off

I feel naive when I think of it now,
how carelessly I stood before him,

like a ballet dancer in a dressing room
bright with the backs of other girls.

This was before the coldness he nursed
and kept warm between his thighs.

I waited too long for a thaw—he waited too.
Taking him into my mouth, I knew the ache

of winter. I heard the silences
grow as a field of stones between us.

When I look back at my body, young
in the bedroom dark, lit by a perpetual city,

I am gripping a rock in my right hand
and he is gripping a rock in his right hand.

We face each other, muscles poised for sex
or war. Who dropped the rock?

Who cast it? I'm unsure,
even now, who cried *mercy* first.

After the _____, time turned like a mood ring.
My mood changed like a thunderstruck sky. The sky
changed like a breast, engorged, staining the front
of a white silk blouse. I got laid off. I went thirteen days
without wearing a bra. I changed my mind about
the fiction of money. Money changed hands. I washed
my hands religiously. Religion changed into sunlight—
something allowed to touch my face. My face changed
into my mother's. No, into a mask of my mother's face.
Traces of heartache changed into a pain in my right hip.
The stock market dipped. The S&P fell freely. I did not
fall to my knees, promising to change my life.
The price of paper towels changed and the price
of toilet paper and the price of white bread and milk.
Whiteness did not change. Some things stayed
the same. We named the moon for its changes, but
it remained the same. Gravity pulled at my organs
like the moon's tug makes a king tide. America's king
would inevitably change and inevitably stay the same.

Resembling Flowers Resembling Weeds

I'm fourteen and the smell of singed hair
circles me like the halo of a pre-Renaissance
Madonna. Loss already on my face.
A summer crush holds out his fingers

for the other boys to smell. The next day
I choose a cute outfit: shorts with tiny
repeating flowers. I braid my hair

into a wreath of juniper and dandelion.
There's an iteration of myself with gills
and fins, who my twin brother knew
as well as he knew himself, then

there's me with petals on my thighs
and in my hair, flowers even inside.
The untrained eye can mistake yarrow

for flower or blue-eyed grass for weed.
Facing the mirror, irises grow wide
across the field of myself. They're so good
at making use of holes. I want to balance

pitchers of seawater on my head. I want
to be more like my eyes. I carry holes
and purses and a picture of me, age six,

Easter bonnet tied under my chin, shins
grazed by bluebells, a steeple I can hear
beyond the frame. An image I've held
in another's retelling. The scentless girl

I was has a fragrance I recognize
in the mirror. The girl and I bring
our rose-perfumed wrists to the flesh

below the ears. Flesh that will one day be eaten
but not consumed. What is covered now by cloth
and petals will be taken wholly. A tongue,
feeling like many, will coax woman out of us.

Of Being in Motion

There's a body marching toward mine.
I can feel its breasts and stomach, hot

against my back. Its breath in my hair.
I accumulate bodies—my own.

The tattoo braceleting my wrist.
My earlobe like a pin hole camera.

My vagina, untouched. My vagina,
stretched. So many bodies treading

toward the others. And the bruises I conceal
with makeup and denial. The scars I inflict

on myself, and the ones I contort
with a mirror to see. I didn't always know

we'd be joined like this—that I couldn't
leave any of myself behind.

In Trisha Brown's *Spanish Dance*
a performer raises both arms like a bailora

and shifts her weight from hip to hip, knee
to knee, ankle to ankle, until she softly

collides with another dancer. The two travel
forward, pelvis to sacrum, stylized fingers

flared overhead, until they meet a third woman
and touch her back like stacked spoons.

Dressed in identical white pants and long
sleeves, the dancers repeat the steps

until, single file, five women shuffle
forward—they go no further.

The dance lasts the exact length of Bob Dylan's
rendition of "Early Mornin' Rain."

How many versions of myself pile
into the others, arms lifted in surrender,

torsos twisting to the harmonica?
But the dancers—I'm moved by their strange

conga line. A train of women traversing
the stage, running gently into a wall.

After the laughter subsided the crying kept after we held hands
and screamed and screamed and squeezed and screamed after
regret and shame and a single bush filled with speckled thrushes
singing redwing bluebird wood thrush on the wood of a branch
and forest thrush in the branches of a forest open pine
and after your mother refused to haunt your dreams after
you placed her in a wooden coffin and you sang like a blue bird
breast trembling beak open like a mother's beak foraging feeding
offspring after lying on a clutch of blue eggs and after spring
after pining for spring ignorant of your grief and unraveling
with or without your blessing cool days and rain after icicles
crying and after you kept from crying and after you cried
there was no one left to protect after you blessed the demon
possessing you and after it left you were even more alone
a grandala calling and calling and after calling after your mother
a hole closed and a hole opened after that after all of that.

Heaven as Olympic Spa

Koreatown, Los Angeles

Gwendolyn Brooks stood stark naked.
I stared into her bespectacled eyes.

Ms. Brooks showed me how
to tend to myself by scrubbing dead skin

with a coarse wash cloth, rinsing
the body's detritus down a common drain.

My flesh was taut, loose,
and dying. Even in paradise I was dying.

At first, this surprised me. Oh, the capsized
boat of the body, Wanda Coleman sighed.

We keep sailing, even when we believe
we're ashore. Coleman drifted to sleep

on the heated jade floor. Clasping
my spa-provided robe, I lay on my side

beside her. Do the dead
dream? I wondered to myself.

Wrong question, Coleman muttered.
I remembered sleeping beside my mother,

touching her nightgown lightly,
as if a gesture could restore the cord

that, in the beginning, tethered us. As if
I smelled her death in the satin scarf

keeping the plastic curlers in place,
or in the Vaseline glossing her arms.

In childhood, I pined for my mother
though she was there.

Here, in the afterlife, I had no mind
to search for her. I was freed

from a loss that haunted me
even before it occurred.

Gwendolyn Brooks hummed a wordless
song that stripped me of all longing.

I untied the robe's stiff belt
and walked amongst the nude women,

my skin brushed smooth and silent.
I was ordinary and motherless.

Because I was not alone,
my nakedness felt unremarkable.

I didn't miss my mother—
I didn't miss missing her.

IV.

INTERVIEWER:

I have one last question: Who is in that mirror?

MICKALENE THOMAS:

It's always me. Sometimes it's also my mother,
my grandmother, or my great-grandmother.
Sometimes it's a person I've never seen before,
sometimes it's the person I want to be . . .
or someone I haven't become yet.

Bluest Nude

1.

When my mother was pregnant, she drove
every night to the Gulf of Mexico.
Leaving her keys and a towel on the shore,
she waded into the surf. Floating
naked, on her back, turquoise waves
hemming her ears, she allowed
the water to do the carrying. It isn't
true. My mother lived hours inland

and her doctor prescribed bed rest. I want her
to be weightless, belly up and moon-lit
or filling a bathtub with hot water and stepping
gingerly, so as not to slip, easing herself
into the cramped tub, rimmed
with dirt from her husband and son,
soaking for as many minutes as she could,
savoring the water as it turned cold.

2.

In the news, there was another

incident . . . If I describe how

the officer treated

the young woman's body,

I am also describing

the color of her body.

Let me refuse simile.

I do not wish to write it.

3.

In the flower of my body—
        blossoms belonging,
                at last,
                        to me,
        sovereign
        place, where I am no one
        but myself: peony and cracked vase,
                        weeping beech and spiraled shell,
                        siren, matron, Jezebel—

a rush of bees enters me,
and I am not stung;

petals unfold in night's
bluest hymn.

4.

The blue swimming pool. The blue
in a record's groove, revolving.
The pink hydrangea turned
powder blue. Glory-of-the-snow

blue. Blue-black blue. The blue
of a bruise. Wild blueberry
blue. The blue you pick. The blue
you choose. The blue that bucks us
like a bull. The blue bowl full
of lilacs. The blue that falls
as tufts of hair from the barber's
chair. The blue sun makes.
The blue shade of a yellow pine.
Television blue. Cadmium blue.
Blue twisted into the spools
of your DNA, forking into two
directions. Blue darkening
your knees. The blue you miss
because—though it almost
killed you—blue was,
for a season, your home.

5.

There was another . . . incident.

If I describe how the officer treated

the young woman's body, I am also

describing the color

of my body.

6.

Then the last piece, a solemn veil lifted
        and tossed to the floor. I know the history
of my body is a pair of hacked off hands

playing the piano. Day after day in the artist's
        studio, I smell the melon's ripe decay.
I draw a second body, then a third, and so on.

My bodies reveal nothing and conceal
        nothing. Pin-up beauty, runaway, Venus
of the Circus Act, nightwalker, wet nurse,

odalisque, reclining nude. The women are me
        and are not only me. Ours are the only eyes.
We construct our seeing as clay or wood

into figurines of air. We perceive their shapes
        and uses just as wind is seen by watching leaves.
These are the paintings I make of myself.

Art is drawn on the cave of my body.
        There are as many walls inside me
as there are bones at the bottom of the sea.

It matters little how small I am in the pool
        of another's eye. It's awe or indifference
I crave. I want to be seen clearly or not at all.

The moon is an eye flung open, useless
        without a pupil. It soothes me, this not seeing.
Painters have gone blind staring at the sun.

At the center of a hurricane is an eye,
        in the midst of which one believes
the storm is over. A woman's face can break,

fall as quickly as night. Sometimes, when I cry,
        all of the eyes which are mine—painted, sketched,
photographed—begin to shed blue tears. I catch them

in my hands or with pots and pans. Or let them fall
        as drifts of snow. I eat them by the fistful.
When you look at me, in our most intimate

exchanges, you drape my nakedness
        in a fabric I neither sewed nor bought. You pin
my beauty with a tack against the wall, or me against

a four-poster bed: thighs splayed, nipples spilling
        spoiled milk. In every light, the fact of history
strips me blue. These are the conditions. The point is

to go on. Drawing myself, as water from a well,
        I can no longer believe in an innocence
that was never mine. It is impossible to draw

a self-portrait without the other women figured
        onto my flesh like barnacles fixed to a gray whale.
I am rough to touch. I am the yellow song

of a blue pain. The women and I walk
        a tightrope of night. Our eyes adjust to growing
darkness. We make of our vision: knowingness.

It's love the women and I make. Love fashions
        our sight. We drink from the Waters That Were
Once Snow. We are quenched and we are thirsty.

Bathers with a Turtle

Three nudes crudely drawn. One crouching,
back turned, right hand feeding the turtle

of the painting's title; another sitting, as if in a chair,
head bowed, eyes downcast; and a central

figure, standing, chewing her hands. My hands
want to take hers—wet with spit, nicked red

and bitten—into mine. It's her ugliness I can't
resist. Or her misery. My gaze keeps returning

to her haunted face: how she is consumed
with herself, how she consumes herself.

It's the kind of dream, every dream, when all
the characters are you. There's something

I've been gnawing: some fleshy part of myself.
It smells like dirt puddled with rain. It boasts

cartilage and fingers. It drifts to my mouth
like a cigarette, a habit. My father is an addict.

He crouches inside me, back turned—it's been
years since I've seen the scars on his cheeks.

He feeds the part of me armored with a carapace.
As a girl, I savored beer he sipped

from a sweaty bottle. I drank what he offered—
not caring if it reminded me of piss—

the glass rim warm with breath. I tasted
what would sour. When I was an infant,

my father softened grapes with his teeth. I ate
from his fingers. Still, though they fed me,

I do not want to hold them. The seated figure tucks
her hands between her thighs. I want to kiss

her knuckles. What I could have been, what I could
become, and what I am squat—naked

and shivering—in the air-conditioned gallery.
All the green and blue mixed to make my flesh.

The guard signals for my attention: Move back,
Miss, behind the line, you're too close to the painting.

Slow Drag with Branches of Pine

Here I am, holding one more

mirror. This time smoke, winding

like a river. I close my eyes,

not because the smoke stings—it

does—but because it's a way

to examine myself, like looking

at your face in a river certain it is not

your face. The smoke combs

like a mother through my hair

or like searching the shoreline

for shells unbroken. I sing to myself

and the smoke drags my voice on its back

just as the breeze heaves it.

Here, in my half-singing,

I'm reminded how to slow drag.

I watch the pine trees creak

and sway. Here, I am

my own twin. I rest my cheek

against my cheek; I barely move at all.

Lotioning My Mother's Back

Because she lives alone and my hands reach
where hers can't, she asks of me this favor.

It is narrow and soft, my mother's back.
When I massage in small circles, my mother

circles her own mother, who is made
of whatever makes a shadow thin

and ungraspable. She wants to touch her.
The bones under my mother's skin—ribcage,

scapula, spine—feel like sharp winter rain.
Between the clouds, I see a patch of sky, glimpse

my aging body: moles like a flicker
of paint, undersides of half-covered breasts,

patches of eczema my fingers soothe
with heavy cream. Is this what a laying on of hands

means? Once my mother touched a garment
and said, full of an awe full of sadness,

She touched this, her skin was inside of this.
My mother's back shines

like the hands I wipe on the towel's face.
Weren't miracles always beginning this way?

Aubade

after Romare Bearden's Patchwork Quilt *(1969)*

My back is turned from him again,
but this time I'm not hunched
over the quilt—his rough thumbs
gripping my waist—I'm standing
in the middle of a room constructed
with pencil, adhesive, and paper.
One foot in the basin, I will scrub
his cigarette hands and yellow eyes
off my skin. I will clean my sex
and start again. Another will come
and I'll forget the coat hung gently
on the hook—different than the way
he took me. He shook like a startled
fish caught in a great blue heron's beak.
Yes, a woman of my kind
has seen the sea. The first time, I gasped
at its glistening mouth.
Endlessly the waves replaced themselves.
I launder my nakedness like a uniform
with water from the pitcher.
Soon another will arrive who I will
wash away. There is a man who dares
to face me, he considers
every angle. He built my form
with precise lines and foraged scraps
of brown. From the harsh shape
my elbow makes, the builder knows
this is a portrait of work,

not pleasure. I love how softly
he touches me, though all I want
is to be left, to spend a morning in bed
alone with the images of dream.

A Family Woven Like Night through Trees

The man asks, *Do you have a family?* My thinking
brushes the air between us like a wet mark

stains white paper. My mother's mother, dead
twenty-two years. A stone house. The ants I've killed.

Robyne, who, when someone hurls
toward me a small cruelty, cries. Memphis in August.

My twin brother crunching ice. All the cousins
I've made. Walking amongst cedar trees.

New Yorkers on New Year's Day or on the first day
of spring. Not children I've birthed, but dead

leaves raked into prickly hills, made messy
with our falling. Artists skinny-dipping

in the ocean at night. It was family
that surged and fell away. But the ties

my grandfather wore on Sundays are kite tails
in my closet. The mums my mother planted

are tiny, decadent flames. Family returns
like a son, the way a wave is always and never

the same. For once, it is not about the body.
I listened as my friend's urge to kill herself grew

clamorous as a field of bells. She stank of it.
Her voice reeked, streaked with ringing—and

as if she were wreathed in baby's breath,
cloaked in a robe of dianthus, as if

she'd been washed by a river stripped
of silt and mud, I drew her close, inhaled

her musk, and brought her brow to mine.
I mean to say, her blood was mine.

Etymology of a Mood

Sometimes I feel like a goddess
with many hands . . . except human.
One hand is amber-gloved, dripping
with honey, and two constantly shoo
the flies. Two hands play "Miss
Mary Mack" while two pairs clap
to "Rockin' Robin." In my hand
a dictionary, in my hand the ash
of want, in my hand a tea cup
whose emptying bears my face,
in my hands a firefly, a sprig
of rosemary between thumb
and forefinger, in my hand
a pinwheel resembling the dahlias
in my hand. What is the word
for this feeling? What is the root
of that word? Tell me
what to call a twin who survives
the other—not *widow*, not
orphan—and why light
defines a shadow. Tell me what year
the sun will fail or when the word *moons*
began to convey the passage
of time. Sometimes I fall asleep
petting my hair with six hands.
By now, all the hairs in this house
are mine. At night I hear
the spider's velvet legs crossing
the web that, if disturbed,

will stick to the fingers of one
of my hands. My right hand
holds a bell the left hand rings.
The last of my hands: I am wringing.

Poem After an Iteration of a Painting by Lynette Yiadom-Boakye, Destroyed by the Artist Herself

A few times a week, Yiadom-Boakye
painstakingly cuts oil paintings she believes
aren't up to snuff. Instead of re-priming
the canvas, she reduces it to 2 X 2 ½ meter
pieces. She begins again. This isn't
an ars poetica. Once, I made love in daylight.

It was a Saturday or Sunday in November
or July. My lover and I stumbled toward
the bedroom, turning our mouths
and our stalk-like waists. I don't remember
if I undressed myself. The edge of the bed felt
precipitous. I've forgotten almost everything

about that day except the competing limbs
of kissing, walking, fucking—how confused
my feet were until, at last, they did not
touch the floor. It was my fault, I wanted so
little. This is not a love poem. Not a catalogue
of attempts. Yiadom-Boakye doesn't set her figures

in time or place. They are composites of photographs,
magazine cut-outs, and the occasional life drawing.
She doesn't call them *portraits*. When she scissors
her failures into unmendable bits, she aims
to deter scavengers and thieves.
In the room where I write this, my hands

smell like Ginger Gold apples. For hours,
I've been looking out the window—staring
into the hallway we took to my bedroom. I know
the sky is a blue wall. I know the walls
were sky blue. Memory paints them yellow.
I'll keep this revision. The rest I've thrown away.

Head on Ice #5

after Lorna Simpson

She's cold as a snake
She'll cut you
She was dreaming
Her face had been cut out of a magazine
Of ice formations
The color of sapphire
She wasn't cut out to be a housewife
She undressed in the middle of the night
She wasn't cut out to be a soccer mom
She was hot
And kicked off the covers
She saw him disappear by the river
She peeled the apple skin
Into one long ribbon
Until she lay naked
In the grass
She wasn't cut out to be a den mother
Her hands were cold
Only to discount her memory
She's cold-hearted
She'd always wanted ice sculptures
At her wedding
They asked her to tell
What happened
Of swans
Her hands were carved from ice
They asked her to tell what happened
Only to discount
Her memory

At least
He didn't
Cut her face
She wore a sapphire ring
Because
You know
All that trouble with diamonds
The jeweler spoke of a classic cut
She was cold-blooded
Memory fell like a bang
Over her eye
She was streaked with melting
On her head
She wore a glacier
Drifting
Like a wig

After a Year of Forgetting

Now I will learn how to tie an apron and unclasp
my bra from behind. I will become hard,
like a moss-covered rock. I'll be stiff as a nightgown

dried on the line. When the pond freezes over, I'll walk
to its center and lie face up until it is May
and I am floating. I'll become an anchor
pitched skyward. I will steer chiseled ships,

spinning fortune's splintered wheel. I will worry
over damp stones. I will clean ash
from the Madonna's cheek using the wet

rag of my tongue. I'll make myself shrine-like
and porcelain; I will stand still as a broken clock.
I will be sore from lovemaking. I will become so large,
my hair, loosened, will be mistaken for the swallow's cave.

After June, there is a year of forgetting, after the forgetting,
antlers adorn the parlor walls. Then it snows, and I'll be
coarse. I'll be soft as my mother's teeth. I'll be sugar crystals

and feathery snow. I'll be fine. I will melt.
I will make children from office paper. They'll be cut
from my stomach wearing blank faces. Bald
and silent, they will come out of me: triplicates

holding hands. I will smooth their foreheads
with a cool iron. I will fold the tepid laundry, turn down
the sheets, then sleepwalk along the Mississippi

until it is ocean and I'm its muddy saint. I will baptize
myself in silt and December. I will become
a pungent, earthly bulb. I'll pillar to salt. I'll remember
the pain of childbirth, remember being born.

There is a scar near my right eye no lover ever noticed
or kissed, a faint mark: split skin sewn.
And so, and now, there was never a *before*. Never
a time when the wind did not smell of dust
or storm or brine or blood. Never an hour when I entered
a field of bluebells without trampling at least one flower.
And so, and then, on the day I was born, a stampede
of horses filled my chest. Astronomers can only guess
how the universe formed. The planet is dying:
the horses, the mothers, the farmers, the bees. I am
the ground, its many grasses and wild clover.
My teeth grow yellow, ache, decay. I wash a plate,
polishing the moon's face—both will outlast my brutal
hands. And so, in the minutes of *after*, the moon drips
on a silver rack and the plate floats, cracked with age,
in outer space . . . a stray soapsud sparkles then bursts.

Notes

Epigraph 1: "Olympia's Maid: Reclaiming Black Female Subjectivity" by Lorraine O'Grady.

"Seeing and Being Seen": In full, the Susan Sontag quote from *On Photography* reads, "A photograph passes for incontrovertible proof that a given thing happened." The Elizabeth Bishop quotation is from "In the Waiting Room."

"Poem After Betye Saar's *The Liberation of Aunt Jemima*": The engine of the poem and the concluding italicized phrases are taken from the spiritual "Down by the Riverside."

"She Said": Italicized and quoted language in this poem are taken from the transcript in "Testimony of the Rape Trial of 1612" from *Artemisia Gentileschi* by Mary D. Garrard and Dr. Christine Blasey Ford's written testimony delivered to the United States Senate Judiciary Committee on September 26, 2018 which concludes with the sentence: "At this point, I will do my best to answer your questions."

Epigraph 2: Interview, Carrie Mae Weems by Dawoud Bey. *BOMB Magazine* July 1, 2009.

"Burying Seeds": Some italicized language in this poem is from Ossie Davis's eulogy of Malcolm X delivered on February 27, 1965 at the Faith Temple Church of God and Christ in Harlem, other italicized lines come from an interview of Betty Shabazz by Mal Goode of ABC News, conducted shortly after her husband's assassination.

"Facing Off": The image of the young woman and man holding rocks is a quotation from the photograph *Combat des amis avec pierres* (1976) by Malick Sidibé.

"Bathers with a Turtle" is after a painting with the same title by Henri Matisse.

Epigraph 3: Interview, Mickalene Thomas by Sean Landers. *BOMB Magazine* July 1, 2011.

"Bluest Nude": Section six lines 3-4 remembers a fictionalized description of Jeanne Duval by Angela Carter in *Black Venus*, quoted by Griselda Pollock in *Differencing the Canon: Revision, Critical Studies in the History and Theory of Art*.

Acknowledgments

Gratitude to the root systems: public libraries, literary journals, small presses, and independent booksellers. In particular, I offer immense thanks to the editors, staff, and readers of the following publications where these poems first appeared:

Academy of American Poets Poem-a-Day: "Primordial Mirror"

Atlantic: "Why I Left the Garden"

Common: "Bluest Nude," "Burying Seeds," "Of Being in Motion," and "On Seeing and Being Seen"

Georgia Review: "Etymology of a Mood" and "Lotioning My Mother's Back"

Gulf Coast: "Diamondback" and "Slow Drag with Branches of Pine" (as "Self-Portrait with Branches of Pine")

Massachusetts Review: "Poem After an Iteration of a Painting by Lynette Yiadom-Boakye, Destroyed by the Artist Herself"

Narrative Magazine: "Two Girls Bathing"

Prairie Schooner: "A Family Woven Like Night Through Trees," "At the Fish House," and "Posing Nude"

Southampton Review: "After a Year of Forgetting"

Southern Indiana Review: "Marigolds of Fire"

Tin House: "Blueprint"

Virginia Quarterly Review: "Aubade," "Bathers with a Turtle," "Heaven as Olympic Spa," and "Resembling Flowers Resembling Weeds"

Yale Review: "[After the_____, I yearned to be reckless. To smash]," "[After the _____, I mothered my mother,]," "[After the _____, I had the urge to dance]," "[After the _____, time turned like a mood ring.]," "[After the laughter subsided the crying kept after we held hands]," and "[There is a scar near my right eye no lover ever noticed]" (as "After the Apocalypse")

A selection of these poems appears in *Blood of the Air*, winner of the 2020 Drinking Gourd Chapbook Poetry Prize, published by Northwestern·University Press.

"After the Apocalypse" appeared in *Together in a Sudden Strangeness: America's Poets Respond to the Pandemic* edited by Alice Quinn and was reprinted in the *Best American Poetry 2021* edited by Tracy K. Smith.

"Burying Seeds" appeared as the featured poem on Poetry Daily, June 26, 2020 and was reprinted in *Why I Wrote This Poem* edited by William Walsh.

"Facing Off" originally appeared in the anthology *Plume Poetry 9* edited by Daniel Lawless.

"Labor" originally appeared in the anthology *I Know What's Best for You* edited by Shelly Oria.

"Resembling Flowers Resembling Weeds" was reprinted in
Furious Flower: Seeding the Future of African-American Poetry
edited by Joanne V. Gabbin and Lauren K. Alleyne.

"She Said" was reprinted in *Verso / vol. 7.*

Gratitude to Natasha Trethewey for selecting "Etymology of a
Mood" for the *Georgia Review*'s 2018 Loraine Williams Poetry
Prize and John Hennessy for selecting "Burying Seeds" for the
2019 DISQUIET Literary Prize in poetry.

Gratitude for the offerings of nourishment and solitude that
greatly shaped this book: Lesley Williamson and Saltonstall
Foundation; Crosstown Arts; Ann Brady and the Robert
Rauschenberg Foundation; and the kind staff of MacDowell.

I am deeply grateful for support from the Bronx Council on the
Arts; Cave Canem Foundation; the National Endowment of
the Arts; the New York State Council on the Arts, New York
Foundation for the Arts, and New York City Department of
Cultural Affairs; the Oscar Williams and Gene Derwood Fund;
and the Rona Jaffe Foundation.

Flowers of gratitude to Abena Asare, Moira Brennan, Jossalyn
Collado, Ross Gay, Aracelis Girmay, Corey Harrower, Zakia
Henderson-Brown, Mark Kendall, Janet Isserlis, Charleen
McClure, Kamilah Aisha Moon, John Murillo, Maile Ogasawara
Garcia, Christina Olivares, Patrick Rosal, Mary Ruefle, Victoria
Sanz, Nicole Sealey, Matthew Shenoda, Evie Shockley, Lyrae Van
Clief-Stefanon, Elizabeth Velazquez, Robyne Walker-Murphy,
Michelle Whittaker, Susan Wilcox, and Jenny Xie for every
variety of wonder, support, shelter, and care.

To each dear friend who cheered me on: thank you, truly, for being in my life. To beloveds and strangers who shared my poems with beloveds and strangers: thank you.

Gratitude to those who provided significant feedback on poems not included here, but whose eyes instructed my hand: especially Charif Shanahan, who spread my poems across his living room floor, and Donika Kelly, who walks with me.

I would like to thank Kwame Dawes for his generous reading and response to the first draft of *Bluest Nude*.

To Ada Limón, Tracy K. Smith, and Mary Szybist: I am exceedingly grateful for the care you took with *Bluest Nude*. Your poems move me. Your poems still me. A single word from you means the world. To Ellen Gallagher, who hands I needed to touch this book, thank you for your generosity, artistry, confidence, and time.

Thanks to the entire Milkweed team for the care, attention, and labor lavished onto this book. Gratitude to Mary Austin Speaker whose advocacy and eye shaped its materiality.

Simone Leigh is an artist I admire beyond measure. I am humbled and honored to have an image of her sculpture on this cover. Thank you, Simone, for trusting my work with yours.

I humbly place *Bluest Nude* into the rippling wake of ongoing conversation, scholarship, and artistry. Particularly, I am indebted to Denise Murrell's *Posing Modernity: The Black Model from Manet and Matisse to Today* and Lorraine O'Grady's "Olympia's Maid: Reclaiming Black Female Subjectivity."

Hand-over-heart gratitude to my schools: Mrs. Perry, Jacqueline Jones LaMon, Tracy K. Smith, Myronn Hardy, Marilyn Nelson, Cornelius Eady, Toi Derricotte, Carl Phillips, Ed Roberson, Terrance Hayes, Natasha Trethewey, Claudia Rankine, Chris Abani, Gregory Pardlo, Vievee Francis, Rachel Zucker, Sharon Olds, Yusef Komunyakaa, Edward Hirsch, Rowan Ricardo Phillips, Meghan O'Rourke, Sally Wen Mao, and all my workshop-mates and instructors at Cave Canem, Callaloo Creative Writing Workshop, New York University's Creative Writing Program, and beyond. Again, to Terrance, bird on my shoulder. And to Gregory and Vievee for "seeing me clearly."

Gratitude to those who raised me with love: my parents and brothers, my aunts and tribe.To my grandparents and way makers, thank you. To my mother: dedication and sunflowers.

Thank you, Dear Reader. May whatever water is found in these pages quench you and make you thirsty.

AMA CODJOE is the author of *Blood of the Air*, winner of the Drinking Gourd Chapbook Poetry Prize. Her honors include a 2017 Rona Jaffe Foundation Writer's Award, a Creative Writing Fellowship from the National Endowment for the Arts, a NYSCA/NYFA Artist Fellowship, and a Jerome Hill Artist Fellowship. Codjoe's work has twice appeared in the *Best American Poetry* series. She lives in New York City.

Milkweed Editions, an independent nonprofit publisher, gratefully acknowledges sustaining support from our Board of Directors; the Alan B. Slifka Foundation and its president, Riva Ariella Ritvo-Slifka; the Amazon Literary Partnership; the Ballard Spahr Foundation; *Copper Nickel*; the McKnight Foundation; the National Endowment for the Arts; the National Poetry Series; the Target Foundation; and other generous contributions from foundations, corporations, and individuals. Also, this activity is made possible by the voters of Minnesota through a Minnesota State Arts Board Operating Support grant, thanks to a legislative appropriation from the arts and cultural heritage fund. For a full listing of Milkweed Editions supporters, please visit milkweed.org.

milkweed
EDITIONS

Founded as a nonprofit organization in 1980, Milkweed Editions is an independent publisher. Our mission is to identify, nurture, and publish transformative literature, and build an engaged community around it.

Milkweed Editions is based in Bdé Óta Othúŋwe (Minneapolis) within Mní Sota Makhóčhe, the traditional homeland of the Dakhóta people. Residing here since time immemorial, Dakhóta people still call Mní Sota Makhóčhe home, with four federally recognized Dakhóta nations and many more Dakhóta people residing in what is now the state of Minnesota. Due to continued legacies of colonization, genocide, and forced removal, generations of Dakhóta people remain disenfranchised from their traditional homeland. Presently, Mní Sota Makhóčhe has become a refuge and home for many Indigenous nations and peoples, including seven federally recognized Ojibwe nations. We humbly encourage our readers to reflect upon the historical legacies held in the lands they occupy.

milkweed.org

Interior design by Tijqua Daiker and Mary Austin Speaker
Typeset in Caslon

Adobe Caslon Pro was created by Carol Twombly
for Adobe Systems in 1990. Her design was inspired by
the family of typefaces cut by the celebrated engraver
William Caslon I, whose family foundry served
England with clean, elegant type from the early
Enlightenment through the turn of the
twentieth century.